CW01064584

Original title:
Beyond the Human Predicament

Copyright © 2024 Swan Charm Publishing

Editor: Jessica Elisabeth Luik
Author: Aurelia Lende
ISBN HARDBACK: 978-9916-759-06-6
ISBN PAPERBACK: 978-9916-759-07-3

The Unfurling Light

In morning's grace, the dawn unfurls,
A tapestry of dreams untwine.
Soft whispers dance with golden swirls,
Awakening the heart's design.

Each ray a promise, gentle, bright,
To guide the weary soul anew.
Through shadows cast in darkest night,
A beacon steady, clear, and true.

The twilight fades, a silent muse,
As light unfurls its tender grace.
In every glow, a path to choose,
And hope reflected in each face.

Transcendent Echoes

Upon the winds, the echoes ride,
Transcending time and fleeting form.
Their whispers bring the past beside,
In gentle waves, in quiet storm.

They tell of love, of joys once known,
Of laughter shared and tears of gold.
In echoes far, a truth is shown,
A story timelessly retold.

Through valleys deep and mountains high,
These echoes weave a bridge of sound.
In every breath, a whispered tie,
A bond eternal, hallowed, profound.

Luminescent Quest

On paths unknown, beneath the skies,
A quest begins with silent might.
Through shadows deep and whispered sighs,
We seek the glimmers of the night.

Each star a guide, each moon a friend,
Illuminates the way we roam.
In luminescent quests, we blend,
In search of heart, in search of home.

With every step, a story grows,
In lights that shimmer, softly pressed.
Through night's embrace, the journey shows,
A luminescent quest, our best.

The Timeless Echo

Amidst the halls where memories blend,
Beyond the clock's relentless chime,
An echo whispers, without end,
A touch of past through realms of time.

In ancient stone, in whispered breeze,
The timeless echo sings its song.
In moments caught 'tween sigh and ease,
A history, both brief and long.

Through every phase, in dusk or dawn,
This echo dances, pure and free.
In timeless breaths, where dreams are drawn,
We find our place in eternity.

Dreams of Infinity

In the cradle of night, stars weep silver tears,
Boundless realms whisper through countless years.

Dreams weave a tapestry, vast and grand,
Where endless horizons by moonlight stand.

Galactic seas stretch with radiant grace,
Beyond mortal reach, creation's embrace.

Worlds within worlds, a celestial art,
Confined in infinity, pure from the heart.

In stillness they spiral, eternal and free,
With dreams of infinity, in cosmic spree.

Cosmic Destinies

Comets blaze trails through oceans of night,
Guiding souls where darkness turns to light.

Timeless echoes through the void resound,
Where celestial bodies in their orbits abound.

Galaxies whisper secrets arcane,
Fates intertwined in a cosmic domain.

Star-born dust, a saga so grand,
Shapes destinies etched by time's gentle hand.

In the fabric of space, destinies merge,
Calling us forth to the cosmic surge.

Mankind's Echo

Ancient stars dim but still hold lore,
Tales of mankind whisper evermore.

From stardust born, to stardust return,
The echo of lifetimes ceaselessly burn.

Through struggles and triumphs, a path we tread,
Voices of ancestors in our head.

Bound by history, futures unfold,
In mankind's echo, the brave and bold.

Infinite night, yet dreams take flight,
Within human spirit, eternal light.

Ethereal Horizons

Morning light gleams on misty bounds,
Ethereal hues where silence surrounds.

Horizons whisper secrets untold,
Luminescent dreams in splendor unfold.

Soft winds carry the scent of stars,
Caressing souls, healing ancient scars.

Boundless skies in a symphony grand,
Painted horizons by unseen hands.

In the twilight of dusk, worlds unite,
Ethereal horizons embrace the night.

Chronicles of the Infinite

In realms beyond our sight,
Where stars weave tales in flight,
Ethereal whispers chant,
Of dreams both bold and slight.

Each galaxy a tome,
Of quests that daring roam,
Through cosmic seas they glide,
In search of distant home.

Memories of the far,
Engraved in every star,
Chronicles of endless space,
Stretch out both near and far.

Planets spin their yarn,
In patterns lost to time,
Their stories intertwined,
In verses so sublime.

Eternal lore remains,
In the celestial veins,
A universe of wonders,
Where the infinite reigns.

Nocturnal Frontiers

The moonlight casts its spell,
In silence night does dwell,
On dreams it softly treads,
In places none can tell.

Stars scatter in the sky,
Like fireflies they lie,
On the canvas of the night,
Their glimmers never shy.

Whispers of the dark,
Embrace the shadows stark,
Exploring realms unseen,
Where mysteries embark.

Night's frontier expands,
In moonlit silent lands,
Unraveling hidden truths,
Beneath the starry hands.

Ethereal night's embrace,
In shadows we find grace,
Nocturnal worlds await,
Their secrets to unlace.

Metaphysical Journeys

Beyond the physical plane,
A journey to ordain,
On paths of spirit laced,
Where mysteries obtain.

Questions of the soul,
In endless oceans roll,
Through realms of thought we sift,
To seek our final goal.

Consciousness expands,
In time's eternal bands,
Exploring Dali's dreams,
In metaphysical lands.

Visions clear and bright,
In the metaphysical light,
We travel inward vast,
In search of higher sight.

Journeys never end,
As souls and thoughts transcend,
Through metaphysical streams,
Inwards they softly wend.

Veiled Realms

In shadows' soft embrace,
Lies a hidden place,
Where dreams and fears collide,
In the veiled realm's face.

Mysteries unfurl,
In twilight's quiet swirl,
An echo of the unknown,
Beyond the waking world.

Secrets deeply kept,
Where whispered thoughts have crept,
In the layers of the night,
Through dreams where we have slept.

Illusions subtly blend,
In realms where time can bend,
Veiled within the unseen,
Where endless paths extend.

In these realms we find,
The echoes of the mind,
Exploring hidden truths,
In shadows intertwined.

Human Ascendancy

In shadows cast by ancient light,
We rise above, we take our flight.
With courage forged in deepest night,
We blaze the trail for human might.

From whispered dreams of yesteryears,
We gather strength and face our fears.
Unbroken will through blood and tears,
We build a path that perseveres.

Our hearts ignite with boundless flame,
Through trials faced, we stake our claim.
In unity, we share one name,
The human spirit, none can tame.

Journey to the Unknown

Beneath the stars, we find our way,
Through dawn's first light and dusk's soft gray.
To lands unseen, where dreams hold sway,
We chase the night, till break of day.

A whispered wind, a silent call,
Through worlds beyond, we risk the fall.
In quest for truth, we break the wall,
Embrace the new, forsake the thrall.

With every step, the path unfolds,
As stories told, our future molds.
We leave behind what once we told,
For in the unknown, courage holds.

Whispers of Forever

In twilight's hush, where night meets day,
There lies a realm where shadows play.
Soft whispers of forever stay,
In silken dreams that gently sway.

Through veils of time, we softly wend,
To realms where hearts do never rend.
In endless dance, where souls transcend,
And moments stretch, they never end.

Our voices blend in silent song,
Though distant yet, they feel so strong.
In whispers soft, we all belong,
To forever's tune, we move along.

Ascending Realms

From earth to sky, we dare to tread,
On stardust paths where angels' tread.
In realms alight, where dreams are fed,
We rise and leave our worldly dread.

With wings of thought, we soar above,
To places kissed by ancient love.
In endless fields, where spirits rove,
We find the peace we're dreaming of.

Ascending realms, our souls ignite,
With truths unseen by mortal sight.
In harmony, both day and night,
We dwell in realms of purest light.

As Stars Collide

In the vastness where galaxies spin,
Two stars on a fated track begin,
Their luminescent trails entwine,
Eternal dance in cosmic design.

Gravity pulls hearts to the core,
As radiant pulses ignite folklore,
Across the void in silent swoon,
Their fiery kiss lights up the moon.

Nebulae whisper ancient lore,
Of celestial love that seeks no more,
In their explosion, creation's song,
Begins anew where souls belong.

Universes Unfold

In darkened skies where silence reigns,
Existence stirs in hidden veins,
A tapestry of boundless threads,
Where time and space in twilight weds.

Unseen forces weave and mold,
Dimensions birthed, stories told,
Galaxies in tender glow,
Infinite realms in ebb and flow.

Mysteries pulse through every fold,
As cosmic tales slowly unfold,
Through stardust trails and ancient light,
Universes born from endless night.

Ascendance

Through shadowed paths, a journey's start,
A quest of soul, of mind, of heart,
Ascending peaks where dreams reside,
In realms where endless skies abide.

Beneath the stars, through nebulae,
Guided by a celestial sway,
Each step a bridge to higher space,
A dance with time in silent grace.

Embracing light, shedding the old,
Transformed by truths the cosmos told,
To ascend is to find one's place,
In the ever-expanding embrace.

Quantum Souls

In quantum realms where particles sway,
Souls dance in a mysterious way,
Entangled hearts in cosmic play,
Bound beyond the dawn of day.

Across the voids where photons gleam,
Their whispers form a silent theme,
Connections spark through waves unseen,
In the fabric of a timeless dream.

Eternal echo in each wave,
Through spacetime's vast and endless maze,
Quantum souls in harmony,
Resonate through infinity.

Celestial Pathways

Through stardust rivers we shall glide,
To realms where constellations hide.
In twilight's glow our spirits soar,
On wings of light forevermore.

The moonlit tides of lucid dreams,
Illuminate our cosmic streams.
A dance of galaxies entwined,
An endless journey through the mind.

Whispers of the Milky Way,
Guide us through the night and day.
Each twinkling light a beacon true,
In skies of midnight's deepest hue.

Reflections of Infinity

In mirrors vast of endless night,
Echoes soft of stellar light.
Reflections dance on silver seas,
Of cosmic sighs and astral breeze.

Infinite skies stretch far and wide,
In them our shadows intertwine.
We drift in realms of spaceless time,
Eternal rhythms, silent chime.

With eyes anew embrace the skies,
Where timeless wonder never dies.
In every star a story told,
Of dreams and light that fate unfolds.

Eternal Whispers

Soft whispers of an ancient song,
Through twilight winds they drift along.
From ages past they softly rise,
A serenade to moonlit skies.

In tender murmurs secrets spin,
Of world unseen and lives within.
Time's gentle breath, a fleeting sigh,
Echos in the heavens high.

The night enfolds its silent grace,
In whispers of a bygone space.
Through starlit paths our souls do weave,
Where dusk and dawn their magic leave.

Boundless Horizons

On edges of the waking sun,
Where dreams and daylight form as one.
Horizons vast in silence gleam,
A canvas wide of life and dream.

Beyond the hills, through valleys deep,
Our wanderlust in shadows creep.
A world unveiled in every dawn,
With hopes reborn, we journey on.

The boundless sky, a sea untamed,
Our spirits free, forever claimed.
In endless flight our hearts will roam,
Through boundless horizons, seeking home.

Radiance Unfurled

In morning's light, the world unfurls,
Golden beams on dew-kissed pearls.
Nature's song in whispers grand,
Paints a wonder across the land.

In twilight's glow, shadows play,
Chasing dreams of night and day.
Stars alight on velvet skies,
Radiance flows where peace lies.

Fields of green, valleys deep,
Light and shadow dance and leap.
Mountains high, oceans wide,
Within their beauty, truths abide.

Moments pass, yet linger on,
Day and night, dusk to dawn.
Time flows gently, whispers heard,
Eternal light, softly stirred.

Eternal Awakening

In the cradle of the night,
Dreams take wing, hearts take flight.
Softly waking, dawn unfurls,
Casting gems in fiery swirls.

Whispers of the morning breeze,
Rustle leaves in ancient trees.
Eyes behold the waking light,
Chasing echoes of the night.

Mountains rise with steadfast grace,
Touching skies, an endless space.
Rivers flow with songs of old,
Stories of the brave retold.

Here we stand, at night's farewell,
In the silence, secrets dwell.
Awakening, a dance anew,
Promise in each morning's hue.

The Cosmic Key

Stars align in cosmic grace,
Tracks of stardust we embrace.
Galaxies whisper ancient tales,
Through space and time, love prevails.

Wonders of the night unfold,
Brilliant stories yet untold.
Constellations, bright arrayed,
Guide us on a path well laid.

Nebulas in colors bright,
Paint the tapestry of night.
Planets twirl in perfect sync,
Mysteries that make us think.

In the vastness, we explore,
Cosmic secrets to adore.
With each key, a door reveals,
Endless wonder, no appeal.

The Everlasting Pulse

Heartbeat of the Earth resounds,
Echoing through all surrounds.
Life in rhythm, pulse so true,
Nature's dance in every hue.

Forests stretch their verdant arms,
Whispers soft, and countless charms.
Rivers pulse with life anew,
Seas of green and skies so blue.

Mountains rise in endless quest,
Reaching for the heavens' crest.
Valleys echo tales of yore,
Songs and stories evermore.

In each pulse, a dream takes flight,
Carrying visions to the night.
Everlasting, pure and grand,
Heartbeat of this timeless land.

Celestial Reflections

Upon the glassy lake's embrace,
Stars sprinkle dreams of ancient grace,
Moonlight whispers, soft caress,
Night unveils its pure finesse.

Constellations waltz on high,
Mirrored worlds beneath the sky,
Reflections weave a silent song,
Eternal dance where hearts belong.

Echoes of the cosmic thread,
Drawn to realms where time is shed,
In the waters, truths unfold,
Mystic tales the heavens hold.

Galaxies bow down to see,
Their splendor in tranquility,
Beneath, above, a boundless sea,
United in their harmony.

As dawn approaches, fades the night,
Reflections linger in the light,
Remembered in the sun's first gleam,
Traces of a starry dream.

Interstellar Longings

Amidst the void where stars are born,
In darkened space, hearts find their morn,
Glow of planets, whispering spark,
Guides us through the endless dark.

Wanderers in search of dawn,
Ancient paths we step upon,
Cosmic bonds we yearn to find,
In the silence, intertwined.

Galaxies with secrets old,
Stories of the brave and bold,
Mysteries of interstellar dreams,
Flowing in celestial streams.

Infinite horizon's tide,
Carry hearts both far and wide,
Stardust trails past worlds unknown,
A voyage where our souls have flown.

Amidst the stars, our longing's thread,
Interwoven, never dead,
In the cosmos, vast and deep,
Our eternal love to keep.

Portal to Forever

In the forest's twilight glow,
A hidden path 'twixt trees and snow,
Opens wide a portal rare,
Leading to the boundless air.

Stepping through the arch of light,
Welcome to the endless night,
Stars ignite the velvet sky,
Lift us where the dreams can fly.

Timeless whispers softly tell,
Of realms where planets weave a spell,
Parallel to mortal time,
Rhythms of the divine rhyme.

Boundless seas of twilight foam,
Show the way to our true home,
Through the portal, visions vast,
Echoes of a timeless past.

Journey through the ages now,
Every star a sacred vow,
In this portal, we have found,
For eternity, we're bound.

Realms of the Stars

Beneath the sky's infinite seams,
Lie kingdoms made of wistful dreams,
Realms of stars, forever bright,
Guardians of the silent night.

Nebulae with mystic hues,
Compose celestial avenues,
Galaxies as sentinels stand,
Watchers of the astral land.

Comets trail their fiery grace,
Through the realms of endless space,
Marking paths where legends blend,
Stories told from end to end.

Planets hum their ancient song,
In this cosmic dance belong,
Orbiting in measured grace,
Echoes in the starry lace.

In these realms, our spirits soar,
Dreams of what lies yet in store,
Voyaging through light and time,
In verse and journey, we align.

Celestial Embrace

Stars enkindle the velvet night,
Guiding hearts with gleam so bright.
Moonbeams weave, through shadows waltz,
Celestial dance, no fleeting faults.

Nebulae whisper tales untold,
Across the skies, their secrets unfold.
Galactic arms in vast embrace,
Draw constellations into space.

Planets hum their cosmic tune,
In perfect orbit 'neath the moon.
Eclipses paint the darkest dream,
In twilight's silent, mystic seam.

The Infinite Horizon

Beyond the hills, where sky meets sea,
Lies a world, unchained and free.
Horizons stretch to realms unknown,
A boundless path, by winds overblown.

Sailors venture, with hope's decree,
Chasing sunrises, longing to see.
Distant lands, with whispers sweet,
Where earth and heavens softly meet.

Footsteps mark the endless quest,
Eyes on horizons, hearts attest.
To find the edge, where dreams reside,
On infinite waves, let spirits glide.

Echoes of Eternity

Time's gentle flow, an endless stream,
Memories drift, like a distant dream.
Echoes of past, soft and profound,
In the heart's chambers, quietly found.

A clock's soft tick, a whispered rhyme,
Marking steps in eternal time.
Moments eternal, fleeting yet grand,
Life's intricate, vast, endless sand.

In silence deep, eternity speaks,
Through valleys low, and mountain peaks.
The echo lingers, resonating clear,
Binding eternity, both far and near.

Soulful Transcendence

In depths profound, the soul takes flight,
Transcending bounds, towards the light.
Silent whispers guide hearts true,
On journeys vast, among skies blue.

Through trials faced, the spirit soars,
Unlocking ancient, hidden doors.
Mystic realms, beyond the sight,
Where souls embrace eternal might.

Serenity's breeze, a gentle sway,
Leading forth by night and day.
In transcendence, souls entwine,
Eternal harmony, pure and divine.

Horizons Eternal

Bright horizons call us near,
Whispers through the skies so clear,
Endless realms of dreams we chase,
In the sun's warm, vast embrace.

Oceans dance with rhythmic grace,
Stars align in cosmic space,
Paths of gold and fields of green,
Wonders woven, yet unseen.

Each dawn paints a new day's light,
Vanishing the lingering night,
Hope renewed with every ray,
Guides our hearts along the way.

Mountains tall and valleys deep,
Hold the secrets that they keep,
Journeys marked by steps unknown,
In this life, we're not alone.

Sunsets whisper sweet goodbyes,
Promising the moon to rise,
Eternal is the quest we ride,
With the universe, we glide.

Celestial Lullabies

Stars above, they softly hum,
Lullabies that gently come,
Cradle moons within the sky,
As the night begins to fly.

Dreams awaken in the night,
Constellations shining bright,
Mystic tales of ancient lore,
Secrets of the stars' encore.

Twilight whispers through the air,
Ethereal, beyond compare,
Every twinkle, every glow,
Sings a song we long to know.

Galaxies in silent sway,
Guide us in their gentle way,
In this dance of space and time,
Heaven's rhythm, pure and prime.

Midnight's kiss upon the brow,
Opens realms, unknown till now,
Celestial tunes, tenderly,
Sing us into dreams so free.

Immortal Paths

Timeless roads beneath our feet,
Where the fates of mortals meet,
Each step taken lays a mark,
In the void, a fleeting spark.

Eons drift on wings so light,
Guiding through the endless night,
Whispers of the ages past,
In the present shadows cast.

Echoes of a distant call,
Lead us onward through it all,
Legends carved in stone and sand,
Crossing every bound and land.

Hearts united, hands entwine,
Soul's resolve as stars align,
In this dance of life and death,
Each one takes another's breath.

Paths of immortality,
Woven into destiny,
With each rise and each descent,
Eternal is the path we tread.

Spectral Paths

Through mist and shadowed trees,
We venture forth unseen,
On spectral paths that breeze,
Where silence is serene.

Ghostly whispers call,
Beyond the moonlit pane,
Drawing us to fall,
Into the night's domain.

With every step we float,
Above the earthly ground,
In dreams our hearts devote,
To echoes that confound.

Wisps of time unfold,
In twilight's gentle grasp,
Revealing tales untold,
Where visions firmly clasp.

Our journey never ends,
On spectral paths we bind,
Where spirit with light blends,
In shadows we will find.

Elysian Promises

Beneath the sky so wide,
Where dreams embark and soar,
Elysian promises abide,
Upon a distant shore.

Whispers of the wind,
Carry hopes anew,
In lands where sorrows mend,
And stars weave through the blue.

Fields of endless light,
Stretch beyond the mind,
In every secret flight,
True peace we seek to find.

Amidst the golden streams,
Our spirits rise and gleam,
In realms of timeless dreams,
Our hearts in sheer esteem.

Elysian realms will call,
Through every life we roam,
In their eternal thrall,
We find our truest home.

Galactic Horizons

Beyond the earthly bounds,
Galactic lights unfold,
Where endless space surrounds,
Stories yet untold.

Stars like diamonds glint,
In the velvet night,
Each a cosmic hint,
Of celestial sight.

Planets in their dance,
Orbit through the vast,
In a timeless trance,
Future, present, past.

Galactic breezes sweep,
Carrying cosmic songs,
Through the void so deep,
Where eternity belongs.

As we gaze in awe,
At horizons wide,
The universe is law,
Our dreams with it abide.

Astral Reveries

In the quiet of the night,
When stars begin to speak,
Astral reveries take flight,
In minds both bold and meek.

Nebulas paint the skies,
With colors soft and bright,
In them our spirit flies,
On wings of purest light.

Constellations weave,
Tales of ancient lore,
In their lines we believe,
And long for legends more.

Moonlight softly drapes,
Across the silent land,
In dreams our heart escapes,
To places vastly grand.

Astral realms invite,
When all the world is still,
In reveries of night,
We wander at our will.

Celestial Odyssey

Under a vast and velvet sky,
Stars whisper tales from far and nigh,
Galaxies twirl in cosmic play,
Guiding souls on their astral way.

Nebulae in colors bright,
Weave a tapestry of night,
Spirits sail on stardust streams,
Beyond the realm of waking dreams.

Planets dance in silent grace,
Marking time through endless space,
Wanderers of the universe,
Bound by fate, for better or worse.

Comets blaze their fleeting trails,
Messages in cosmic gales,
Whispers of the past and more,
Secrets from creation's core.

Among the stars, our hearts align,
In the infinite, divine,
Exploring realms so far apart,
Yet always close within the heart.

Infinite Reflections

Mirror of the endless sea,
Reflects the sky's eternity,
A dance of light, of ebb and flow,
In its depths, all secrets know.

Ripples cast on water's skin,
Echoes of what lies within,
Whispers of a distant shore,
Journals of what came before.

Mountains tall and valleys deep,
In reflections, secrets keep,
Infinite the worlds they show,
Parallel in hidden glow.

Time suspended in the glass,
Moments never meant to pass,
Through each gaze, a different tale,
Past and future, intersperse.

Though we stand on constant ground,
In reflections, worlds are found,
Endless in their silent plight,
Infinite beyond our sight.

Radiant Transcendence

Light that breaks the dawn anew,
Paints the sky in golden hue,
Transforms the night to vibrant day,
Chasing shadows far away.

Through the prism, light divides,
Colors burst as darkness hides,
A spectrum of pure, radiant beams,
Igniting hearts with hopeful dreams.

In the glow, paths clear and true,
Spirits lift, and souls renew,
Transcending bounds of earthly ties,
Soaring through the boundless skies.

Within every shaft of light,
Lies a spark of endless might,
A power to transform and guide,
From the depths where fears reside.

Radiant the world becomes,
As light transcends, as vision comes,
To every soul, a shining flame,
Eternal, bright, and without name.

The Uncharted Realm

Beyond the maps, where dragons sleep,
Lies a land, both wide and deep,
Uncharted by the human eye,
Hidden beneath the azure sky.

Forests ancient, wild and free,
Guard their secrets silently,
Paths unmarked by mortal feet,
Where the wild and wondrous meet.

Oceans vast with waves untamed,
Whisper names that none have named,
Creatures of the deep unknown,
In this realm, their spirits roam.

Mountains rise to touch the stars,
In their shadows, hidden scars,
Tales of old and futures bright,
In this realm beyond our sight.

Adventurers, both brave and bold,
Seek this land of myths untold,
To chart the course through dreams and fears,
In the uncharted of our years.

Splendor of the Stars

Through the veil of twilight's tender grace,
Glisten spheres in a silent chase.
Guardians of the night they embrace,
Whispers of secrets across space.

Their glowing fires paint the sky,
Witnesses to eons passing by.
Crafting dreams where hopes lie,
In their presence, hearts fly.

Tiny lanterns in the vast dark,
Guiding souls with a silent spark.
Through their light, we embark,
On journeys where mysteries lark.

Galaxies swirl in a dance so grand,
Eternal waltz, perfectly planned.
In this cosmic expanse, we stand,
Awed by the wonders unspanned.

Under their shimmer, we find might,
A testament to the endless night.
Stars above, our guiding light,
In their brilliance, our spirits take flight.

Infinite Endeavors

Mountains high and valleys low,
To horizons where we go.
Through the storms and the glow,
Chasing dreams, steady flow.

In the heart of challenge we dive,
Through the struggles, we strive.
Every moment fully alive,
In our essence, we thrive.

Bridges built from hope so strong,
Paths unknown, we belong.
With a spirit enduring and long,
To the future, we are drawn.

In our quests, together we stand,
Hand in hand across the land.
Infinite endeavors completely planned,
In unity, creations are unplanned.

With courage lit and eyes so wide,
Challenge the world with every stride.
Embrace the journey as a guide,
In each endeavor, stars collide.

The Whispering Cosmos

Across the vast and silent sea,
Speaks the cosmos, wild and free.
In whispers, they decree,
Songs of the everlasting spree.

Nebulas painting skies with art,
Galactic wonders, infinite chart.
In their whispers, we take heart,
A dance where dreams embark.

Planets in their timeless orbits sway,
Through silent night and golden day.
In their paths, we find our way,
In their whispering tapestry, we stay.

Void and light in perfect sonnet,
Tales untold in their bonnet.
Through the cosmos, we are on it,
A journey, infinite upon it.

Stars that speak in silent prose,
To the universe, the heart it knows.
In their whispers, beauty grows,
In the cosmos, eternal repose.

Human Resonance

Through the echoes of ancient past,
Resonates a spirit, strong and vast.
In every heart, moments fast,
Human essence meant to last.

In struggles faced and battles won,
Underneath the timeless sun.
Together, we forge as one,
In unity, humanity is spun.

Dreams that soar above the clouds,
Through the silent, cheering crowds.
We are voices, clear and loud,
In resonance, beautifully proud.

Bridges of kindness we create,
In love and joy, resonate.
Hand in hand, hearts elate,
In togetherness, we find fate.

Through the ages, clear and true,
Human spirit old and new.
In every soul a sky so blue,
In resonance, forever we renew.

Ephemeral Legacies

Footprints in the sands of time,
Fade away, yet leave a trace.
Moments fleeting, nature's rhyme,
In hearts and minds, they find their place.

Whispers of a bygone age,
Echo softly, tales retold.
History scrawls on life's stage,
In shadows, truths enfold.

Dewdrops on a morning leaf,
Mirror lives, so brief, so bright.
Time's caress, both joy and grief,
Dances in the soft moonlight.

Ephemeral as the dawn,
Yet in essence, forever known.
Legacies, though swiftly gone,
In spirit, deeply sown.

Shall we chase the fleeting hours,
Or embrace the life's embrace?
Ephemeral, and yet ours,
In each breath, find our grace.

Celestial Symphony

Stars compose a cosmic tune,
In the night, their voices blend.
Beneath the silver crescent moon,
Galactic melodies suspend.

Orion's belt keeps steady time,
To a rhythm, ageless, pure.
Planets swing in graceful rhyme,
In a dance that shall endure.

Nebulae weave a silent song,
Colors burst in opal streams.
In their light, our souls belong,
Dreaming ancient, star-born dreams.

Comets trace their fiery arcs,
Through the vast, uncharted sea.
In their glow, eternal sparks,
Guide us to infinity.

Listen to the cosmic choir,
Symphony of endless night.
In the stars, our hearts aspire,
To the heavens, take our flight.

Galactic Footprints

Galactic pathways, vast and wide,
Footprints left in stardust trails.
Across the void, where dreams abide,
In the silence, mystery sails.

Cosmic winds, a gentle breeze,
Whisper secrets of creation.
Galaxies spark like autumn leaves,
Dancing in divine elation.

Planets orbit, timeless glides,
Mark the endless cosmic walk.
In their whispers, truth resides,
Among the stars, the ancients talk.

Telescopes, our windows bright,
Gaze into the past, afar.
Tracing paths of ancient light,
Dreams enshrined in every star.

Minds and hearts, in wonderment,
Trace these footprints in the skies.
Galactic trails, omnipresent,
In their patterns, wisdom lies.

Continuum's Call

In the river of time, we flow,
Moments weave, a tapestry.
Endless currents, to and fro,
Guide us through eternity.

Every second, rich with chance,
Life unfolds in measured beat.
Continuum's rhythmic dance,
Marches on with tireless feet.

Past and future, meld as one,
In the present, secrets lie.
Underneath the timeless sun,
Echoes of the ages sigh.

Universes in a blink,
Spin their tales in cosmic swirls.
In these patterns, let us think,
Of the boundless, endless whirls.

Continuum's call softly hums,
In our souls, its chords embrace.
From its flow, creation drums,
Life's eternal, boundless grace.

Across Time's Veil

Through mists of ages, whispers glide,
Ephemeral threads, time's secrets hide,
Echoes of dreams, from dusk till dawn,
In veils of night, lost moments drawn.

Stars trace stories, ancient and new,
Binding hearts, in memories true,
Time's river flows, relentless, deep,
Guarding tales that shadows keep.

Embers of love, across the years,
Burn bright through joy and flowing tears,
In clocks that spin, and suns that fall,
We find our place, we heed the call.

Footsteps fade, yet linger still,
On paths long worn, by strength of will,
Through every age, and every tale,
We journey on, across time's veil.

Realities Converged

In realms where dreams and truths entwine,
Dimensions merge, in perfect line,
Shattered mirrors, reflect as one,
A tapestry, of light and sun.

Alternate paths, like rivers blend,
In unseen worlds, where thoughts suspend,
Futures dance, on edges keen,
Converging hues, of what has been.

Across the void, minds intertwine,
Creating fates, both yours and mine,
Parallel echoes, calling clear,
In twilight's glow, we stand, revere.

Through veils unseen, our truths unfold,
Revealing secrets, stories bold,
In symphonies, of realms profound,
Our souls converge, in visions found.

Pathways Eternal

In forests deep, and mountains high,
Where ancient roads, to nowhere lie,
Eternal paths, through time's vast scape,
Guide wanderers to destiny's gate.

From dawn's first light, to twilight's fall,
Whispered paths, both great and small,
In every footstep, story's told,
In every turn, a journey bold.

Cobbled ways, through history's heart,
Crafted by hands, that played their part,
Silent trails, through time's embrace,
Lead souls to realms, of endless grace.

In shadows cast, and sunlit beams,
Pathways stretch, in waking dreams,
Guiding steps, on roads unknown,
Through ages past, and futures sown.

Celestial Nexus

Beneath the stars, where dreams ignite,
A nexus born, of cosmic light,
Galaxies spin, in endless dance,
In celestial realms, we find our chance.

Nebulae bloom, in radiant glow,
Through the universe, our souls flow,
Connections forged, in starlit skies,
In astral seas, where spirits rise.

Planets whisper, ancient lore,
Of lives entwined, forevermore,
In constellations, stories weave,
Our hearts in cosmic webs, believe.

Through spacetime's veil, we drift, we soar,
In interstellar love's encore,
From worlds afar, to nexus near,
Our destinies align, crystal clear.

Celestial Mirrors

Upon the still of night they shine,
Reflecting dreams through endless time.
Stars whisper secrets, softly bright,
Guiding lost souls towards the light.

In cosmic dance, they weave with grace,
A mirror to the vast embrace.
Beyond the bounds of space and lore,
They speak of worlds unknown, obscure.

Moonlit shadows play their part,
Echoing the celestial heart.
Galaxies sing their ancient hymns,
A symphony on stellar rims.

Eternal mirrors in the skies,
Reveal the truths behind our lies.
In silent awe, we gaze above,
Seeking whispers of cosmic love.

Beyond the known, the treasures hide,
In starlit mirrors, they confide.
A universe so vast, so near,
Reflecting dreams we hold dear.

Echoes of Tomorrow

In the whispers of the dawn,
Future echoes softly spawn.
Timeless ripples in the stream,
Paint the patterns of our dream.

From the depths of what may come,
Songs of hope are softly strummed.
Visions clear in twilight's gray,
Mark the paths we'll walk someday.

Through the shadows, light will break,
New beginnings we shall make.
Every heartbeat, every breath,
Echoes paths that lie unsaid.

Winds of change, they gently blow,
Seeds of future they will sow.
Every choice and every sorrow,
Shapes the echoes of tomorrow.

In the quiet, hear the call,
Future echoes beckon all.
With each dawn, the promise grows,
Endless are the paths it shows.

Silent Migrations

In the hush of night's deep sigh,
Wings of dreams begin to fly.
Wanderers of the sky and sea,
Whisper tales of where they've been.

Across the vast and misty plains,
Silent migrations leave no chains.
Guided by a hidden star,
They travel near, they travel far.

Patterns traced in winter skies,
Silent flocks at dawn arise.
From cold whispers to warm lands,
Nature's dance, in unseen hands.

Through the silence, journeys made,
In distant lands, their shadows wade.
Following the ancient trails,
Silent stories, silent sails.

To the unknown, they are drawn,
Guided by the break of dawn.
Across the world's open pages,
Life unfolds in silent stages.

Immortal Whispers

In the quiet of the night,
Whispers rise, eternal light.
From the past and future too,
Voices speak in shades of blue.

Ancient stories carried far,
From a time beyond the stars.
Echoes in the sands of years,
Immortal whispers calm our fears.

Through the ages, shadows blend,
Mystic tales they softly send.
Wisdom flows from ancient days,
Guiding us in countless ways.

Listen close, the whispers speak,
Timeless truths that all hearts seek.
In the stillness of the mind,
Secrets of the soul we find.

Beyond the realms of space and time,
Whispers hold a truth divine.
Eternal voices in the breeze,
Speak of love and endless seas.

The Eternal Ballet

Under moon's gentle, silver glow,
A dance of stars begins to show.
Celestial pirouettes take flight,
In the canvas of the night.

Whispers of the cosmic breeze,
Waltz across the sky with ease.
Galaxies in grand array,
Partake in this ballet.

Nebulae like gowns of gold,
Spinning tales of time untold.
Every twirl, a cosmic thread,
Weaving through the stars, widespread.

Eternal steps in silent sound,
In the vastness so profound.
Unified in cosmic dance,
This ballet, a timeless trance.

With dawn's light, the dance does fade,
To twilight's glowing serenade.
Yet, when night returns in grace,
The stars resume their ancient chase.

Galactic Symphony

In the depths of starry seas,
Where light and time can cease to please,
A symphony begins to play,
Beyond the veil of night and day.

Harmonic waves and cosmic tides,
Compose a song where silence hides.
Planets hum with silent glee,
In this galactic melody.

Blazing comets streak the void,
With chords of fire they have deployed.
Asteroids in rhythm sway,
In the Milky Way's ballet.

Celestial choirs of stars align,
In harmonies that seem divine.
Their glittering notes blend and merge,
In a symphony that cannot urge.

Through the eons, music flows,
In space where time and matter glow,
And each celestial note will be,
A part of this vast symphony.

The Timeless Path

Through forests dense and meadows wide,
Beneath the ancient trees' abide,
There lies a path where time stands still,
And moments linger by their will.

Each step echoes of the past,
Of memories that ever last.
Old folklore etched in stone and leaf,
Whisper tales of joy and grief.

Cobblestones kissed by night's dew,
Bear witness to the ages through.
And in the dawn's first gentle light,
The path continues in its might.

Seasons blend where shadows play,
In this stretch where dreams convey.
Yet, every footprint left behind,
Speaks of journeys intertwined.

To wander here is to embrace,
A world of endless time and space.
The timeless path, forever worn,
A journey where new tales are born.

Beyond Mortal Shadows

Beyond the veil of mortal sight,
Where shadows rule the endless night,
Lies a realm of whispered lore,
Of echoes from the evermore.

Spirits drift on silent air,
In places dark and seldom fair.
Their laments, a haunting song,
In the shadows, they belong.

Whispers cool like morning dew,
Of lives once lived and dreams untrue.
Fleeting shades in twilight's frame,
Ember souls without a name.

Yet beyond the mortal realm,
Where shadows strive to overwhelm,
Light eternal breaks the black,
Guiding lost souls gently back.

In the end, as shadows fade,
Peace resumes, in light displayed.
Beyond the shadows, futures gleam,
Boundless as a waking dream.

Transcendent Tapestry

In threads of light, a story spins,
Weaving dreams through night and day.
Colors blend where life begins,
In a dance where shadows play.

Each stitch tells a whispered tale,
Of hearts united, souls set free.
From the cusp we watch, we sail,
Through a boundless, endless sea.

Golden strands of twilight gleam,
In a tapestry divine.
Every fiber is a dream,
Framed in reverent design.

As we touch the sacred weave,
Feel the patterns softly glow.
Transcending all, we believe,
In the love the threads bestow.

Together we create, entwined,
This masterpiece we cast.
A work of art, pure and refined,
Bound by tapestries of the past.

The Untold Journey

Paths untaken, stars unseen,
Mysteries fold within the night.
Whispers through the might-have-been,
Guide the soul on wings of light.

Mountains rise in silhouette,
Silent echoes call our name.
In the stillness, never met,
Lies a journey wrapped in flame.

Rivers carved by ancient lore,
Canyons hold the secrets deep.
Voices from the distant shore,
In our dreams, they gently seep.

Steps we tread in silent grace,
Carving time like sands of gold.
In the void, we find our place,
In the stories yet untold.

Every twist and every turn,
Leads us closer to the dawn.
In the darkness, we discern,
The path where dreams are drawn.

Awakened Stars

Beneath the velvet sky's embrace,
Stars awaken, gleam and glow.
Whispers in the silent space,
Glimmers in the night bestow.

Constellations paint the night,
Souls ignited, hearts a-flame.
In the stillness, searing bright,
Each a flicker, each a name.

Galaxies in swirls of fire,
We navigate through cosmic streams.
Hearts entwined with pure desire,
Bound by interstellar dreams.

In the vastness, time suspends,
Moments caught in astral beams.
Awakened stars become our friends,
Guardians of our deepest dreams.

Through the endless, starlit dance,
Mysteries of light unfold.
Awakened stars in cloned enhance,
The universe, in brilliance, told.

Harmony of the Ages

Echoes of a timeless song,
Resonate through fields and time.
Voices rise, both weak and strong,
In a harmony sublime.

Ancient rhythms, hearts in sync,
Melodies of old arise.
Through the ages, moments link,
In the music of the skies.

Cymbals clash and flutes take flight,
Choruses of yore and new.
Syncretized in pure delight,
Every note from gold to blue.

From the dawn of whispered tales,
To the twilight's fading hue.
Every story, every wail,
In the symphony renew.

Ancient chords and newborn strains,
Blend in timeless serenades.
Harmony through joy and pains,
In the music of the ages swayed.

Ageless Serenades

In shadows cast by evening's light,
Old tales whisper through the night.
Timeless melodies softly play,
Binding hearts that went astray.

The moonbeams dance on streams below,
A symphony from ages ago.
In every chord, a life once lived,
In tunes, their blessings freely give.

Ancient oaks with stories told,
Branches strong, and roots that hold.
Leaves flutter, like voices raised,
In ageless serenades they praise.

Soft lullabies of distant lands,
Echo softly in the sands.
Time may pass, but love remains,
In ageless serenades, their claims.

Beneath the stars, night's gentle sway,
Music carries dreams away.
To realms where past and present kiss,
An ageless serenade of bliss.

Echoes of Eternity

Beyond horizons, whispers call,
From dreams where shadows oft befall.
Each echo tells a timeless tale,
Of endless love, where hearts prevail.

In skies of twilight's purple hue,
Stars recount what once they knew.
The whispers grow, a gentle breeze,
In echoes of eternity, we seize.

Across the voids of space and time,
Souls immortal, visions climb.
Each life a verse in cosmic rhyme,
Echoes speak of love, sublime.

Mountains hold the secrets deep,
Of promises the world shall keep.
In every stone, a memory's key,
Echoes of eternity set free.

Through lifetimes danced on earth's embrace,
In quiet moments, we retrace.
The echoes of eternity,
Resound in love's infinity.

Stardust Trials

In cosmic seas, we drift afar,
Through nebulas and astral scars.
Each trial faced, a cosmic mile,
In stardust paths, we reconcile.

A journey penned by comet's light,
Through trials wrought in endless night.
Where shadows blend and sparks ignite,
Stardust trials in silent flight.

Galaxies whisper ancient lore,
Of hearts that braved and spirits sore.
In every trial, wisdom finds,
The stardust trails that souls entwine.

Emerald seas of stars above,
Bear witness to our quest for love.
Each trial a step, on stardust ground,
Where dreams are lost and then are found.

Through nebulous fields we come to know,
The trials pass, but we shall grow.
In stardust trials, light prevails,
And to the stars, our spirit sails.

Atlas of Eternity

In every map, a story lies,
Charting lands beneath the skies.
Through deserts vast and oceans deep,
The atlas of eternity we keep.

Mountains high and valleys low,
Crafted by the winds that blow.
Each peak and plain, a timeless trace,
In this atlas, we embrace.

Pages worn by hands of old,
Tales of wonders yet to be told.
In every line, a journey's end,
In eternal maps, we comprehend.

Rivers twist and forests breathe,
Paths untraveled, we perceive.
The atlas guides through mystery,
Tracing lines of history.

In every heart, a map unfolds,
Of dreams pursued and tales of old.
The atlas of eternity,
Charts the course of destiny.

Celestial Dreams

In skies alight with midnight gleam,
Where stars bestow their radiant beams,
We sail on waves of cosmic streams,
Afloat in endless, star-lit realms.

The moon whispers its ancient lore,
Of worlds we've charted, yet adore,
Constellations' glows implore,
To dream forever, evermore.

Galaxies in quiet hush,
Unveil the night with gentle brush,
Painting wonder, sparking lush,
Celestial dreams in tender flush.

Nebulae in colors sway,
Guiding us through night to day,
As endless wishes find their way,
In realms where heart and starlight play.

We rise on waltzes, star-embraced,
On paths the dark and light have traced,
In dreams where stars and futures laced,
A timeless voyage softly paced.

Timeless Echoes

In caverns deep where shadows dwell,
Reside the whispers, stories tell,
Of echoes past, where silence fell,
In timeless waves, their mysteries quelled.

Voices sing in faded tones,
Through ancient halls and earthen stones,
Recounting lives and long-lost groans,
Within these timeless, haunted zones.

Past and present weave as one,
In echoes where the time is spun,
From dawn to dusk, and setting sun,
Their melody, a thread begun.

Listen closely, you shall hear,
The voices neither far nor near,
They call in whispers, crystal clear,
In echoes timeless, drawing near.

From yonder past to future's crest,
They speak of love, of hearts confessed,
Of journeys taken, souls at rest,
In echoes timeless, always blessed.

Everlasting Journeys

From dawn to dusk, the roads extend,
In never-ending, winding blend,
Through valleys deep and mountains' bend,
The journey's call will never end.

With every step, a story told,
Of paths untraveled, long and bold,
In whispers low or voices bold,
Your heart the map, the compass, soul.

Across the seas, beneath the sky,
Where wild winds and storms pass by,
In evergreen glades, we fly,
The journey's pulse our lullaby.

In sunsets' hues or midnight's grace,
We find our path, a boundless space,
Our spirits' dance, a fervent chase,
In endless time and boundless place.

For life itself, a journey grand,
With every touch, with every hand,
In lands unknown or native strand,
Our everlasting journeys stand.

Ephemeral Migrations

As seasons change, the world transforms,
In fleeting hues and whispered forms,
The passage swift, the moment warms,
In migrations, time deforms.

Birds take flight in patterned dance,
Across the skies, an endless trance,
With wings of hope, through distance prance,
Their journey brief, a fleeting chance.

Leaves cascade in golden floods,
Over hills and meadows' spuds,
In rivers, lakes, and forest's buds,
Ephemeral in nature's thuds.

Day to night and dusk to dawn,
Shadows grow and shades withdrawn,
The cycles spin, the moments gone,
In migrations, life's song drawn.

Brief our steps in cosmic scheme,
Like fireflies in twilight's gleam,
Ephemeral migrations dream,
In beauty fleeting, we redeem.

Celestial Meditations

Under vast skies, where stars convene,
Cosmic whispers softly glean,
In the silence, dreams unfold,
Galactic secrets quietly told.

Nebulae dance, in silent grace,
Through the void, they leave a trace,
Planets turn in rhythmic flow,
Eternal patterns, softly glow.

In this realm of endless night,
Constellations breathe in light,
Luminous trails, across the span,
Whisper stories of time's grand plan.

Contemplations, deeply sown,
In star-kissed dreams, I'm not alone,
Ephemeral thoughts, vast and free,
Boundless realms where souls can flee.

Meditations on the sky,
Where infinity meets the eye,
In celestial, endless streams,
The universe reveals its dreams.

Infinite Pilgrimages

Beyond the horizon's ever-crest,
Journeys call, a wandering quest,
Footprints fade, where stories tread,
Endless paths where hearts have led.

Mountains rise, with silent might,
Valleys whisper under night,
Rivers carve their ancient song,
In their courses, we're carried along.

Time weaves tales on pilgrim's way,
Through twilight, and through breaking day,
Every step, a tale rewritten,
In the quest of paths unbidden.

In the leaves, the wind recalls,
Every step that stumbles, falls,
Pilgrimages, vast and true,
Chasing worlds both old and new.

Infinite paths, unknown, unseen,
In this life and in between,
Pilgrims' hearts will always roam,
Seeking places to call home.

Realms Beyond

Through portals of the unseen,
Worlds obscure, in twilight sheen,
Realms beyond our earthly ken,
Haunted shades and spirits' den.

Whispers float on spectral breeze,
Ethereal songs through ancient trees,
Phantoms dance in shadowed light,
In the depths of endless night.

In the mist, where shadows play,
Forgotten echoes find their way,
Realms so distant, yet so near,
In every sigh, a ghostly tear.

Visions of what lies beyond,
Faintly grasped, forever fond,
Dreams intwine with night and dawn,
In realms where mortal bonds are drawn.

seek the places eyes can't see,
In the depths of mystery,
There's a call, a silent plea,
In these realms we'll find the key.

Quantum Visions

Particles dance in quantum state,
Floating through an unseen gate,
Realities woven with a thread,
In the space where time is spread.

Light entwined in wave and crest,
Forms a pattern, never rest,
In the quantum field so vast,
Present, future, echo past.

Mysteries in equations lie,
Boundaries where dimensions sigh,
Quantum leaps in thought and form,
Where known worlds are never norm.

Systems pulse in silent beat,
Parallel worlds around us meet,
In their dance of light and shade,
Quantum visions give parade.

Through the scope of inner sight,
Beyond the veil of day and night,
Hidden realms, they come alive,
In quantum thoughts, we dare to strive.

Ethereal Labyrinths

In realms where shadows twist and lean,
A dance of light, a woven seam,
The echoes whisper, soft and keen,
In labyrinths where phantoms dream.

With every turn, the path unveiled,
Through mist and veils, the spirits hailed,
A journey cloaked, in moonlight trailed,
In labyrinths where time is paled.

The stars above, like sentinels,
In silent watch, their stories tell,
A journey infinite, as spells,
In labyrinths where secrets dwell.

The heart beats on, in sync with night,
In corridors of sheer delight,
A maze of wonder, souls ignite,
In labyrinths of spectral light.

In dreams, the maze will gently fade,
The echoes dim, the shadows wade,
Yet memories in twilight stayed,
In labyrinths where dreams are made.

Beyond Mortal Kin

In realms unseen by mortal eyes,
The cosmic dance of endless skies,
Where whispers of the ancients rise,
Beyond the bounds where fate complies.

A timeless sea of stardust shone,
Amidst the echoes, all alone,
In silence, where the ageless roam,
Beyond the flesh, beyond the bone.

The veil of life, a fleeting gleam,
In shadowed light, the spirits scheme,
A world encased in echoed dreams,
Beyond the mortal, worldly theme.

Eternal night and endless dawn,
In cosmic threads, our lives are drawn,
A tapestry where truths belong,
Beyond the mortal, forever gone.

In quiet realms, where time is thin,
The souls converge and softly grin,
In unity, yet still akin,
To mysteries beyond mortal kin.

Dreamscapes Eternal

Upon the shores of sleep's sweet grace,
Where dreams embark on boundless pace,
The stars align in cosmic lace,
In realms profound, a timeless space.

The night unveils its whispered song,
In shadowed realms, where we belong,
In visions clear, both faint and strong,
In dreamscapes where the heart is drawn.

A journey through the astral mist,
Where fantasies and truths exist,
The soul's desires cannot resist,
In dreamscapes born of fate's own twist.

Each nightly voyage, fresh and new,
In colors bright and depths of blue,
A symphony of thoughts accrue,
In dreamscapes where the spirit flew.

The dawn will break, the dreams will wane,
Yet shadows of their magic reign,
Eternal as the sweet refrain,
In dreamscapes where the heart remains.

Infinite Sojourn

Upon the winds of time we sail,
In endless quest, we blaze the trail,
Through star-lit skies and moonlight pale,
An infinite sojourn prevails.

The cosmos sings its ancient song,
With every beat, we move along,
Through realms unknown, both weak and strong,
An odyssey where souls belong.

The planets dance in rhythmic lines,
In harmony, the cosmos binds,
A journey free from mortal binds,
In infinite sojourn, love defines.

Each moment, like a fleeting star,
A compass guiding from afar,
In boundless seas, no shore can bar,
In infinite sojourns, we are.

No end in sight, no final rest,
In cosmic arms, we find our quest,
Eternal journey, ever blessed,
An infinite sojourn, manifest.

Empyrean Awakenings

In the hush of dawn's first light,
Whispers dance through realms unseen,
Awakening stars from their night,
With secrets only dreams convene.

Celestial choirs gently sing,
Melodies of distant spheres,
In the silence, angels' wings,
Brush against our mortal fears.

From the cosmos, wisdom pours,
Rivers of ethereal glow,
Guiding hearts through unseen doors,
To where boundless visions flow.

Empyrean realms unfold,
Their mysteries soft and deep,
Awakening souls, untold,
Through the realms where seraphs sleep.

Eternal night yields to day,
Stars give way to morning's crest,
In empyrean's soft array,
Hearts awaken, souls find rest.

Celestial Musings

In the canvas of the sky,
Dreams are painted with each star,
Galaxies in hues awry,
Stories told from near and far.

Midnight's whisper, soft and low,
Secrets old, yet ever new,
In the starlit ebb and flow,
Hearts find solace, spirits flew.

Planets dance in silent waltz,
Cosmic rhythms, ancient song,
In their glow, no shadows fault,
Timeless tones where souls belong.

Onto moons, our wishes cast,
Echoed back through time and space,
In their light, the present, past,
Merge within night's warm embrace.

Skyward eyes and hearts ascend,
Celestial musings gently blend,
Infinite dreams, without end,
Astral journeys, we suspend.

Galaxies Within

In the depth of quiet mind,
Galaxies in thought unfurl,
Stars of wisdom, there we find,
Hidden truths, like precious pearl.

Constellations made of dreams,
Illuminate our innermost,
In their light, our spirit gleams,
With knowledge, we're engrossed.

Universe within our soul,
Endless realms of wonder lie,
With each breath, we make them whole,
'Neath the boundless cosmic sky.

Through the ether's vast expanse,
Journeys of the heart begin,
In each thought, we take a chance,
On the galaxies within.

Infinite in our embrace,
Stars of insight gently spin,
Guiding us to inner space,
Galaxies where truths are kin.

Timeless Voyages

Across the seas of endless time,
Voyages of hearts unfold,
In their wake, eternal rhyme,
Stories of the brave and bold.

Through the oceans of the night,
Navigating stars so bright,
Timeless paths, a boundless flight,
Guided by their gentle light.

Horizons call with whispers grand,
Legends of forgotten lands,
In their tales, we place our hand,
With the cosmos, make our stand.

Sails unfurl in cosmic breeze,
Timeless ships on ageless seas,
Bound by naught, our spirits seize,
Boundless dreams carried with ease.

Every voyage, heart's desire,
Fuels the soul's undying fire,
Through the stars, we climb higher,
On timeless quests, we never tire.

Infinite Rhythms

Beneath the cosmic dances, stars align,
In waltzes vast, eternal paths they trace,
A symphony that stretches, old as time,
In silent songs of endless, boundless grace.

Within the ebb and flow of ceaseless tides,
The moon conducts the waves in whispered tones,
An orchestra where chaos calmly bides,
In rhythms carved from pressures of the unknown.

Through forest shade where leaves in twilight sway,
To whispers of the wind they move and bend,
An infinite reel of dusk till breaking day,
Where nature's melodies forever blend.

In hearts that beat in synchrony unseen,
A metronome within our flesh and bone,
The pulse of life, on which our dreams convene,
A cadence where the seeds of hope are sown.

So listen close to echoes of the night,
The rhythms of the universe arise,
In every beat, a tale of cosmic plight,
Infinite rhythms dance before our eyes.

Universal Murmurs

In whispers soft, the galaxies converse,
Their ancient tongues recount creation's tale,
Eclipsing time, in vast and astral verse,
Till stardust dreams before our eyes unveil.

The planets hum in orbits vast and wide,
A language known to only those who see,
Their silent murmurs, secrets they confide,
Unfolding realms of endless mystery.

Beneath the twinkling canopy of night,
A symphony of whispers fills the air,
In cosmic murmurs, faint and out of sight,
Unveiling truths, to those who would dare care.

The comets trace their paths in fleeting blaze,
With tales of yore inscribed in fleeting trails,
Their whispers echo through the starlit haze,
A chronicle of time in cosmic scales.

So lean in close and heed the silent hum,
In murmurs lies the wisdom of the skies,
A universal tongue, so strange, yet numb,
In its embrace, the universe replies.

Temporal Passages

Through winding corridors of fleeting time,
Our moments thread through tapestries unspool,
A journey where unknowns their truths sublime,
And days of yesteryears in echoes pool.

Each second ticks away, a ghostly tread,
In temporal passages, lives interlace,
The future's breath, with whispers softly led,
And memories drift in the void of space.

The present's heartbeat throbs in steady pace,
A metronome of now and here, alive,
In fleeting glances, fleeting to embrace,
A fragile whisper, striving to survive.

In twilight's hush, the past begins to fade,
Yet shadows cast their echoes on the mind,
Through passages where light and dark cascade,
A labyrinth where destinies unwind.

Thus travel we through ebbs of transient flow,
In pathways carved by moments sweet and sore,
To find that time, a tale we scarcely know,
Is but a river's song along the shore.

Unwritten Realms

In pages blank as moon's uncharted face,
A story waits with ink of dreams untold,
Unwritten realms where fantasy we chase,
And weave the threads of mystery to hold.

In shadows cast by worlds we've yet to pen,
The echoes of potential softly speak,
A canvas vast, a sea of might-have-been,
Where whispers of the future's vision peek.

Through realms of thought, where phantoms gently roam,
The quill of fate prepares the next design,
In unfilled tomes, the heart finds shelter, home,
In scribbles that eternity define.

So write in stars, in cosmic calligraphy,
The tales that ne'er another soul has known,
Unwritten realms, where endless freedom's key,
And every dream a seed by winds are sown.

Within the silence of the untouched page,
The whispered hopes of futures yet to dawn,
Unwritten realms, their gates we boldly stage,
In ink and thought, the saga carries on.

Eternity Beckons

Beyond the stars, where silence dwells,
A timeless echo softly swells,
Infinite dreams in cosmic seas,
Whispering truths on astral breeze.

The moonlit paths we dare to tread,
By ancient whispers gently led,
In shadows cast by endless time,
We seek the light, pure and sublime.

Eons flow, a river vast,
Where future blends with faded past,
Each moment shared, a trace of grace,
In love's embrace, we find our place.

Celestial realms, a boundless flight,
Through realms of dark and realms of light,
Eternity beckons, calls our name,
In endless dance, we're all the same.

Echoing hearts in cosmic rhyme,
Transcending space, defying time,
A journey endless, echoes ring,
In boundless love, our spirits sing.

Infinite Tapestries

Threads of fate in cosmic loom,
Weave patterns rich through ancient gloom,
Each story told in warp and weft,
Leaves traces deep, by time bereft.

Colors bright and shadows blend,
In timeless dance, where paths extend,
Infinite tapestries unfold,
In secrets whispered, truths untold.

Stars align in woven light,
Guiding souls through endless night,
Patterns shift in gentle grace,
As universe reveals its face.

Threads of gold and silver gleam,
In fabric of an endless dream,
Through cosmic winds, the threads are spun,
Infinite tales, forever begun.

Tapestries that tie our fate,
In every joy and sorrow's weight,
Infinite realms in every seam,
In woven threads, we find our dream.

Dimensions Adrift

Through portals vast and worlds unknown,
Our spirits drift, untethered, flown,
Dimensions vast in endless sprawl,
We wander realms where echoes call.

In twilight shades and dawn's embrace,
We find our path, our sacred space,
Through shifting planes and stardust streams,
We chase the light that fuels our dreams.

Spectral forms in realms unseen,
Where time's illusion grows serene,
Dimensions adrift, a mystic sea,
Where all that is and was shall be.

On cosmic winds, we sail afar,
Through galaxies and dying stars,
In endless search for fate's design,
Where truth and dreams in wonder bind.

Through realms of dark and endless light,
We journey forth, our spirits bright,
Dimensions adrift, forevermore,
In cosmic dance, our hearts explore.

Cosmic Dance

In the velvet sky above, stars collide,
Whispers of galaxies, vast and wide.
Waltzing on the event horizon's edge,
Planets spin without a pledge.

Nebulae pirouette in radiant hues,
Comets sweep by with ethereal views.
A ballet of light in the void so grand,
Mysteries of space, like drifting sand.

Supernovas burst in shimmering tales,
Through the cosmos, their essence trails.
Dark matter's rhythm, unseen yet profound,
Crafting a melody without sound.

Moondust swirls in cosmic embrace,
Dancing through time, a timeless race.
Eclipses shadow, then reveal,
A universe in perpetual, silent zeal.

Timeless Spirals

In spirals the ancient stars do turn,
Galactic arms in cosmic churn.
Time's river flows, unseen, unfelt,
In endless cycles, all is held.

The past and future twine and blend,
In the grand design, without end.
Every moment, every chance,
Swept in a timeless, cosmic dance.

Black holes anchor the spinning spheres,
Holding secrets of countless years.
Light bends, and reality warps,
In the silent, vast star-filled orbs.

Ancestors of light trace the skies,
Whispers of the cosmos in their eyes.
Echoes of beginnings in every star,
Spirals of time, near and far.

The Boundless Echo

Across the void, a whisper spreads,
Through starry fields, in silken threads.
Boundless echo, timeless roam,
From the heart of space, its eternal home.

Quasars blaze with ancient fire,
Fueling dreams and dark desire.
In the corridors of space, soundless waves,
Secrets of the universe, it saves.

Gravity weaves a silent tune,
Beneath the watchful cosmic moon.
Celestial bodies feel the pull,
Boundless echo, never dull.

Infinite expanse, where light is born,
Cradling stars till the fated morn.
Echoes that everlastingly persist,
In this boundless cosmos, they exist.

Echoes of the Infinite

From the depths of space, an echo springs,
Timeless songs that the cosmos sings.
A call that bridges time's great span,
Infinite whispers of creation's plan.

Auroras dance in spectral hues,
Painting space in ethereal blues.
Galaxies hum their ancient tune,
Beneath the watch of a cosmic moon.

Vast expanses, silent and deep,
Where secrets of the infinite sleep.
Stars echo stories of their birth,
Of the timeless void and ancient mirth.

In the quiet of the endless night,
Where darkness weaves with shards of light.
Echoes of the infinite, softly play,
In the vastness where creation lay.

Whispers of Infinity

In the silence of the night, a gentle breeze flows,
Whispers of infinity, in the cosmos it sows.
Stars align in patterns, mysterious and vast,
Eternal stories of the universe, forever cast.

Oceans dance with moonlight, an ageless ballet,
Currents weave through time, night and day.
Every droplet sings, a hymn of endless rhyme,
In the whispers of infinity, we find the sublime.

Mountains rise with grandeur, touching the sky,
Silent keepers of secrets, as eons pass by.
Their peaks whisper tales, of days long past,
In a language of rocks, forever set and fast.

Forests breathe in union, a harmony so pure,
Every leaf a note, in nature's grand overture.
The wind moves gently, with secrets to impart,
Whispers of infinity, echoing through the heart.

In the dance of creation, lie whispers untold,
Mysteries of existence, in the universe unfold.
Every heartbeat, a pulse, in this grand mystery,
In the whispers of infinity, we find our eternity.

Human Symphony

Voices rise in chorus, a symphony of souls,
Every note a story, as the melody rolls.
In the heartbeats of many, a rhythm so grand,
We play our parts, in a vast, human band.

Eyes meet in silence, sharing untold dreams,
In the spaces between words, truth softly gleams.
Hands reaching out, across time and space,
In the human symphony, we find our grace.

Laughter and sorrow, blend in harmony's weave,
Every echo a testament, to what we believe.
Through trials and triumphs, together we rise,
In the human symphony, strength never lies.

Lives intertwined, like threads in a loom,
Creating patterns of light, amidst the gloom.
In every bond formed, and every tie,
The human symphony, reaches for the sky.

Moments fleeting, yet eternal in their streak,
In the quiet and the chaos, we seek.
Each heartbeat, each breath, a note in time,
In the human symphony, eternally we chime.

Dreams Unfettered

In the quiet of the night, dreams take flight,
Boundless visions, in the realm of twilight.
Colors blend and swirl, in uncharted streams,
In the world of sleep, we live our dreams.

Mountains rise majestically, touching the stars,
Oceans stretch endlessly, erasing the scars.
In dreams unfettered, boundaries dissolve,
Every mystery beckons, inviting to resolve.

We soar with abandon, wings spread wide,
Exploring realms where imagination can't hide.
In fields of wonder, where reality bends,
Dreams unfettered, where the soul ascends.

Through labyrinths of thought, we navigate,
In this sacred space, we liberate.
Every whisper a guide, every vision a seed,
In dreams unfettered, we find what we need.

As dawn approaches, gently stirring the night,
Dreams recede, but leave their light.
In waking hours, their essence we hold,
Dreams unfettered, a story untold.

Ethereal Voyage

In the hush of twilight, a journey begins,
Through realms unseen, where starlight spins.
Ethereal paths, winding like a stream,
A voyage to the heart of every dream.

Silent spheres of light, beckon from afar,
Guiding the voyager, like a shooting star.
In the void so vast, and the spaces between,
Whispers of eternity, softly convene.

Mystic realms unfold, in hues of twilight,
An odyssey of wonder, pure and bright.
In shadows and light, a cosmic ballet,
Ethereal voyage, through the milky way.

Through nebulae and galaxies, the traveler roams,
Across the universe, a journey to unknown homes.
Each star a beacon, each planet a song,
In the ethereal voyage, where souls belong.

In the end, it's not the destination we seek,
But the journey through the timeless and unique.
Every moment a treasure, every heartbeat a guide,
Ethereal voyage, in the cosmos wide.